Simple Pillow /

Just a few easy-to-learn sewing techniques are all you need to create the 10 trendy pillows in this book. Our clear photos and instructions make it simple.

2
10
18
6
4
12
8
14
16
20

LEISURE ARTS, INC. • Maumelle, Arkansas

Burlap Flange Pillow

Finished Pillow Size (including flange)**:** based on size of doily [ours is 21" x 16" (53 cm x 41 cm)]

Yardage is based on 58"/60" (147 cm/152 cm) wide burlap fabric with a usable width of 56" (142 cm) and 43"/44" (109 cm/112 cm) muslin with a usable width of 40" (102 cm).

- ☐ desired size vintage doily [ours is 16" x 11" (41 cm x 28 cm)]
- ☐ burlap fabric for pillow front and back (see **Cutting the Pieces**)
- ☐ muslin **and** polyester fiberfill to make pillow form (see **Cutting the Pieces**) **OR** a purchased pillow form to fit pillow
- ☐ water-soluble fabric marking pen
- ☐ sewing machine zipper foot
- ☐ fabric glue
- ☐ General Supplies (see page 28)

CUTTING THE PIECES

*Follow **Preparing Fabrics**, page 28, to prepare fabrics before cutting pieces. We do not recommend prewashing burlap. All measurements include 1/2" seam allowances.*

From burlap fabric:
- Cut 1 **pillow front** and 1 **pillow back** the size of the doily + 3" on all sides.

From muslin:
- Cut 1 **pillow form front** and 1 **pillow form back** the size of the doily + 2¹/₂" on all sides.

MAKING THE PILLOW

Match right sides and use a 1/2" seam allowance throughout. Backstitch at beginning and ending of stitching line.

1. Center and glue the doily to the **pillow front**; allow to dry.

2. Matching raw edges and leaving an opening for turning along 1 edge, pin and stitch pillow front to **pillow back**, taking 2 stitches diagonally at each corner as shown in **Fig. 12**, page 31. Trim each corner as shown in **Fig. 13**, page 31. Turn pillow right side out; press.

3. To make the flange, use marking pen to draw a line 1/2" from each edge. Leaving an opening parallel to the opening at the outer edge of the pillow, topstitch along drawn line (**Fig. 1**).

Fig. 1

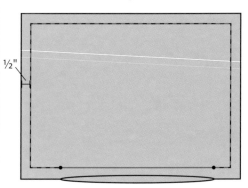

4. If making a pillow form, refer to **Making A Pillow Form**, page 30.

5. Insert pillow form. Close opening at pillow edge using the **Ladder Stitch**, page 31.

6. Attach zipper foot to sewing machine on right side of needle. Stitch inner area closed along remainder of drawn line.

Burlap Flower Pillow

Finished Size: 16" x 16" (41 cm x 41 cm)

SHOPPING LIST

Yardage is based on 58"/60" (147 cm/152 cm) wide burlap fabric with a usable width of 56" (142 cm) and 43"/44" (109 cm/112 cm) muslin with a usable width of 40" (102 cm).

- ☐ ⁷/₈ yd (80 cm) of burlap fabric for pillow front, back, and flower
- ☐ ⁵/₈ yd (57 cm) of muslin **and** polyester fiberfill to make pillow form **OR** a purchased 16" (41 cm) square knife-edge pillow form
- ☐ scrap of brown fabric to cover button
- ☐ 2" (51 mm) diameter covered button kit
- ☐ 2" (51 mm) diameter brown wood 2-hole button
- ☐ 6" (15 cm) upholstery needle
- ☐ extra strong upholstery thread
- ☐ tracing paper
- ☐ General Supplies (see page 28)

CUTTING THE PIECES

*Follow **Preparing Fabrics**, page 28, to prepare fabrics before cutting pieces. We do not recommend prewashing burlap. All measurements include ¹/₂" seam allowances.*

From burlap fabric:
- Cut 2 **pillow fronts** and 1 **pillow back** 17" x 17".
- Trace pattern, page 23, onto tracing paper. Using pattern, cut 2 **flowers**.

From muslin:
- Cut 1 **pillow form front** and 1 **pillow form back** 18" x 18".

MAKING THE PILLOW

Match right sides and use ¹/₂" seam allowances throughout. Backstitch at beginning and ending of stitching line.

1. Matching raw edges, layer **pillow fronts**; baste ¹/₄" from raw edges.

2. Matching raw edges and leaving an opening for turning along 1 side, pin and stitch pillow front to **pillow back**, taking 2 stitches diagonally at each corner as shown in **Fig. 12**, page 31. Trim each corner as shown in **Fig. 13**, page 31. Turn pillow right side out; press.

3. If making a pillow form, refer to **Making A Pillow Form**, page 30.

4. Insert pillow form and close opening using the **Ladder Stitch**, page 31.

5. Using scrap of fabric and covered button kit, follow manufacturer's instructions to make covered button.

6. Alternating points, layer **flowers** in center of pillow front.

7. Refer to **Tufting**, page 31, and use covered button on front and wood button on back to tuft pillow center.

Tied Sash Pillow

Finished Size: 18" x 18" (46 cm x 46 cm)

SHOPPING LIST

Yardage is based on 43"/44" (109 cm/112 cm) wide fabric with a usable width of 40" (102 cm).

☐ ⁵/₈ yd (57 cm) of floral print fabric for pillow front and back

☐ ³/₈ yd (34 cm) of stripe fabric for sash

☐ ⁵/₈ yd (57 cm) of muslin **and** polyester fiberfill to make pillow form **OR** a purchased 18" (46 cm) square knife-edge pillow form

☐ tracing paper

☐ General Supplies (see page 28)

CUTTING THE PIECES

*Follow **Preparing Fabrics**, page 28, to prepare fabrics before cutting pieces. All measurements include ¹/₂" seam allowances.*

From floral print fabric:
• Cut 1 **pillow front** and 1 **pillow back** 19" x 19".

From stripe fabric:
• Cut 2 strips 6" x 25". For **sash**, trace pattern, page 23, onto tracing paper. Using pattern, trim ends of each strip.

From muslin:
• Cut 1 **pillow form front** and 1 **pillow form back** 20" x 20".

MAKING THE PILLOW

Match right sides and use ¹/₂" seam allowances throughout. Backstitch at beginning and ending of stitching line.

1. Matching raw edges and leaving an opening for turning along 1 side, pin and stitch **pillow front** to **pillow back**, taking 2 stitches diagonally at each corner as shown in **Fig. 12**, page 31. Trim each corner as shown in **Fig. 13**, page 31. Turn pillow right side out; press.

2. If making a pillow form, refer to **Making A Pillow Form**, page 30.

3. Insert pillow form and close opening using the **Ladder Stitch**, page 31.

4. Leaving an opening for turning along one long side, sew **sashes** together. Turn right side out; press. Use a Ladder Stitch to sew opening closed.

5. Tie sash around pillow.

Welted Bolster Pillow

Finished Size: 8" diameter x 20" long (20 cm x 51 cm)

SHOPPING LIST

Yardage is based on 54" (137 cm) wide home decorating fabric with a usable width of 52" (132 cm) and 43"/44" (109 cm/112 cm) muslin with a usable width of 40" (102 cm).

- ☐ ³/₄ yd (69 cm) of taupe print fabric
- ☐ 1¹/₂ yds (1.4 m) of silver decorative nail head trim
- ☐ 1⁵/₈ yds (1.5 m) of ⁴/₃₂" (3 mm) diameter cord
- ☐ ³/₄ yd (69 cm) of muslin and polyester fiberfill to make pillow form
- ☐ 1¹/₂" (38 mm) diameter covered button kit to make 2 buttons

- ☐ sewing machine zipper foot
- ☐ hot glue gun and glue sticks
- ☐ 12" (30 cm) upholstery needle
- ☐ extra strong upholstery thread
- ☐ cellophane tape
- ☐ tracing paper
- ☐ General Supplies (see page 28)

CUTTING THE PIECES

*Follow **Preparing Fabrics**, page 28, to prepare fabrics before cutting pieces. All measurements include ⁵/₈" seam allowances.*

From taupe print fabric:
- Cut **pillow** 26³/₈" x 21¹/₄".
- Trace pattern, page 24, onto tracing paper. Using pattern, cut 2 **pillow ends**.

From muslin:
- Cut **pillow form** 26³/₈" x 21¹/₄".
- Using pattern, cut 2 **pillow form ends**.

MAKING THE PILLOW

Match right sides and use ⁵/₈" seam allowances throughout. Backstitch at beginning and ending of stitching line.

1. Matching short edges and leaving an opening for turning in the center, stitch short edges of **pillow** together. Press seam allowances open.

2. Follow **Making and Attaching Welting**, page 29, to make a bias strip 1³/₄" x 58¹/₂" and to make welting. Making clips along the seam allowance, attach welting to each raw edge of pillow. Leave zipper foot on sewing machine.

3. Fold 1 **pillow end** in half; fold in half again. Make a ¹/₄" clip in raw edges at each fold. Fold pillow in half; fold in half again. Make a ¹/₄" clip in raw edges at each fold. Matching clips, sew 1 pillow end to each end of pillow. Turn pillow right side out; press.

4. For pillow form, repeat Steps 1 and 3.

5. Stuff pillow form with fiberfill and close opening using the **Ladder Stitch**, page 31.

6. Insert pillow form and close opening using the Ladder Stitch.

7. Using fabric and covered button kit, follow manufacturer's instructions to make 2 covered buttons.

8. Refer to **Tufting**, page 31, Steps 1-2 to tuft pillow from end to end. You'll need to "scrunch" the pillow to insert needle from end to end. Secure and clip thread.

9. Cut trim in half. Trimming ends as needed, glue a length 4" from each end.

European Pillows

Finished Size: 26" x 26" (66 cm x 66 cm)

Fig. 1

SHOPPING LIST

Yardage and instructions are for making 2 European Pillows. Yardage is based on 43"/44" (109 cm/112 cm) wide fabric with a usable width of 40" (102 cm).

- ☐ 3 1/8 yds (2.9 m) of chevron stripe fabric for large pillow fronts, backs, and ruffles

- ☐ 7/8 yd (80 cm) of red solid fabric for small pillow fronts and flanges

- ☐ 3 1/4 yds (3 m) of muslin **and** polyester fiberfill to make pillow form **OR** 2 purchased 26" (66 cm) square European pillow forms

- ☐ General Supplies (see page 28)

CUTTING THE PIECES

*Follow **Preparing Fabrics**, page 28, to prepare fabrics before cutting pieces. All measurements include 1/2" seam allowances.*

From chevron stripe fabric:

If using directional fabric, be sure to cut fabric so that print is in correct direction for a "right" and "left" pillow.

- Cut 1 *lengthwise* strip 3" x length of fabric. Cut strip in half to make 2 **ruffles**.
- From remaining fabric, cut 2 **large pillow fronts** 18" x 27" and 2 **pillow backs** 27" x 27".

From red solid fabric:

- Cut 2 **small pillow fronts** 10" x 27" and 2 **flanges** 1 3/4" x 27".

From muslin:

- Cut 2 **pillow form fronts** and 2 **pillow form backs** 28" x 28".

MAKING THE PILLOW

Match right sides and use 1/2" seam allowances unless otherwise indicated. Backstitch at beginning and ending of stitching line. If using directional fabric, be sure to sew flange, ruffle, and small pillow front to opposite edges of large pillow front so you have a "right" and "left" pillow.

1. Matching **wrong** sides, press 1 **flange** in half lengthwise.

2. Using a 3/8" seam allowance, baste raw edge of flange to 1 long raw edge of 1 **large pillow front**.

3. Matching **wrong** sides, press **ruffle** in half lengthwise.

4. Leaving 4" of thread free at each end, baste 3/8" and 1/4" from raw edges of ruffle **(Fig. 1)**.

5. Pull bobbin threads until ruffle measures 27". Matching raw edges, pin ruffle to **large pillow front** over flange.

6. Use a 3/8" seam allowance to baste ruffle to large pillow front.

7. With flange and ruffle sandwiched in between, sew **small pillow front** to large pillow front; press.

8. Matching raw edges and leaving an opening for turning along 1 side, pin and stitch pillow front to **pillow back**, taking 2 stitches diagonally at each corner as shown in **Fig. 12**, page 31, and catching ends of ruffle in seams. Trim each corner as shown in **Fig. 13**, page 31. Turn pillow right side out; press.

9. If making a pillow form, refer to **Making A Pillow Form**, page 30.

10. Insert pillow form and close opening using the **Ladder Stitch**, page 31.

11. Repeat Steps 1-10 to make remaining pillow.

Tied Bolster Pillow

Finished Size: 6" diameter x 16" long (15 cm x 41 cm) excluding ends

SHOPPING LIST

Yardage is based on 43"/44" (109 cm/112 cm) wide fabric with a usable width of 40" (102 cm).

- ☐ ⁵/₈ yd (57 cm) of floral print fabric for pillow ends
- ☐ ¹/₄ yd (23 cm) of paisley print fabric for pillow center
- ☐ ¹/₄ yd (23 cm) of pink print fabric for pillow ruffles
- ☐ 1³/₈ yds (1.3 m) of ³/₈" (10 mm) wide pink sheer ribbon for ties
- ☐ ¹/₂ yd (46 cm) of muslin fabric **and** polyester fiberfill to make pillow form **OR** a purchased 6" x 16" (15 cm x 41 cm) bolster pillow form
- ☐ tracing paper
- ☐ General Supplies (see page 28)

CUTTING THE PIECES

*Follow **Preparing Fabrics**, page 28, to prepare fabrics before cutting pieces. All measurements include ¹/₂" seam allowances.*

From floral print fabric:
- Cut 2 **pillow ends** 15" x 20".

From paisley print fabric:
- Cut 1 **pillow center** 7" x 20".

From pink print fabric:
- Cut 2 **ruffles** 3" x 40".

From muslin:
- Cut **pillow form** 16" x 20".
- Trace pattern, page 24, onto tracing paper. Using pattern, cut 2 **pillow form ends**.

MAKING THE PILLOW

Match right sides and use ¹/₂" seam allowances unless otherwise indicated. Backstitch at beginning and ending of stitching line.

1. Matching wrong sides, press 1 **ruffle** in half lengthwise.

2. Leaving 4" of thread free at each end, baste ³/₈" and ¹/₄" from raw edges of ruffle (**Fig. 1**).

Fig. 1

3. Pull bobbin threads until ruffle measures 20". Pin ruffle to one long edge of **pillow center**.

4. Use a ³/₈" seam allowance to baste ruffle to pillow center.

5. Repeat Steps 1-4 with remaining ruffle.

6. With ruffles sandwiched in between, sew 1 long raw edge of **pillow end** to each long raw edge of pillow center; press.

7. Press remaining long raw edge of each pillow end 5¹/₄" to wrong side. Stitch 5" from fold.

8. Sew pillow together along remaining raw edges catching ruffle ends in stitching. Turn pillow right side out; press.

9. Matching short edges and leaving an opening for turning in the center, stitch short edges of muslin **pillow form** together. Press seam allowances open.

10. Fold 1 muslin **pillow form end** in half; fold in half again. At raw edges, make a ¹/₄" clip at each fold. Fold muslin pillow form in half; fold in half again. At raw edges, make a ¹/₄" clip at each fold. Matching clips, sew 1 pillow form end to each end of pillow form.

11. Stuff pillow form with fiberfill and close opening using the **Ladder Stitch**, page 31.

12. Cut ribbon length in half. Insert pillow form; tie a ribbon length around each end over stitching.

Round Welted Pillow

Finished Size: 16" (41 cm) diameter

Yardage is based on 54" (137 cm) wide fabric with a usable width of 52" (132 cm) and 43"/44" (109 cm/112 cm) muslin with a usable width of 40" (102 cm).

- ☐ 5/8 yd (57 cm) of floral print fabric for pillow
- ☐ 5/8 yd (57 cm) of muslin fabric **and** polyester fiberfill to make pillow form **OR** a purchased 16" (41 cm) diameter round pillow form
- ☐ 1 1/2 yds (1.4 m) of 4/32" (3 mm) diameter cord
- ☐ 2" (51 mm) diameter covered button kit to make 2 buttons
- ☐ sewing machine zipper foot
- ☐ 6" (15 cm) upholstery needle
- ☐ extra strong upholstery thread
- ☐ cellophane tape
- ☐ paper for tracing
- ☐ General Supplies (see page 28)

CUTTING THE PIECES

*Follow **Preparing Fabrics**, page 28, to prepare fabrics before cutting pieces. All measurements include seam allowances.*

From floral print fabric:
- Trace pattern, page 25, onto paper. Using pattern, cut **pillow front** and **pillow back**.

From muslin:
- Using pattern, cut **pillow form front** and **pillow form back**.

MAKING THE PILLOW

Match right sides and use 5/8" seam allowances unless otherwise indicated. Backstitch at beginning and ending of stitching line.

1. Follow **Making and Attaching Welting**, page 29, to make a 1 3/4" x 54" bias strip, to make welting and to attach welting to **pillow front**. Leave zipper foot on sewing machine.

2. Matching raw edges, with welting sandwiched in between, and leaving an opening for turning, pin and stitch **pillow back** to pillow front. Clip seam allowances about every 1/2" and turn right side out; press.

3. If making a pillow form, refer to **Making A Pillow Form**, page 30.

4. Insert pillow form and close opening using the **Ladder Stitch**, page 31.

5. Using fabric and covered button kit, follow manufacturer's instructions to make 2 covered buttons; set aside.

6. Refer to **Tufting**, page 31, and use buttons to tuft pillow.

Chalkboard-Look Pillow

Finished Size: 20" x 20" (51 cm x 51 cm)

SHOPPING LIST

Yardage is based on 58"/60" (147 cm/152 cm) wide cotton duck fabric with a usable width of 56" (142 cm) and 43"/44" (109 cm/112 cm) muslin with a usable width of 40" (102 cm).

- ☐ 1$^1/_4$ yds (1.1 m) of black cotton duck fabric for pillow
- ☐ 1$^3/_8$ yds (1.3 m) of muslin fabric **and** polyester fiberfill to make pillow form **OR** a purchased 20" (51 cm) square knife-edge pillow form
- ☐ 2$^1/_2$ yds (2.3 m) of $^4/_{32}$" (3 mm) diameter cord
- ☐ fine-point and medium-point white paint pens
- ☐ white dressmaker's tracing paper
- ☐ sewing machine zipper foot
- ☐ tracing paper
- ☐ cellophane tape
- ☐ General Supplies (see page 28)

CUTTING THE PIECES

*Follow **Preparing Fabrics**, page 28, to prepare fabrics before cutting pieces. All measurements include seam allowances.*

From black cotton duck fabric:
- Cut **pillow front** 23" x 23".
- Cut **pillow back** 21$^1/_4$" x 21$^1/_4$".

From muslin:
- Cut **pillow form front** and **pillow form back** 22$^1/_4$" x 22$^1/_4$".

MAKING THE PILLOW

Match right sides and use a $^5/_8$" seam allowance unless otherwise indicated. Backstitch at beginning and ending of stitching line.

1. Trace pattern, page 26, onto tracing paper. Center and draw a 12" circle around words. Center pattern on **pillow front**; pin. Slide dressmaker's tracing paper under pattern and draw over pattern with a dull pencil, transferring pattern to pillow front.

2. Use the paint pens to "paint" the words and circle and to free-hand the leaves around the circle. Multiple "coats" may be needed for adequate coverage.

3. Centering the design, trim pillow front to 21$^1/_4$" x 21$^1/_4$".

4. Matching wrong sides, fold one corner of pillow front as shown in **Fig. 1**. Measure along folded edge and mark across corner 1" from point. Sew along drawn line. Repeat for each corner. Repeat for **pillow back**.

Fig. 1

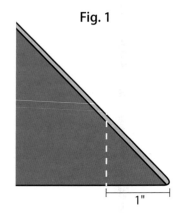

1"

5. Follow **Making and Attaching Welting**, page 29, to make a 1$^3/_4$" x 90" bias strip, to make welting, and to attach welting to pillow front. Leave zipper foot on sewing machine.

6. Matching raw edges and leaving an opening for turning, pin and stitch pillow front to pillow back. Trim each corner as shown in **Fig. 13**, page 31. Turn pillow right side out; press.

7. If making pillow form, refer to **Making A Pillow Form**, page 30.

8. Insert pillow form and close opening using the **Ladder Stitch**, page 31.

It is
Well
with my
Soul

Ruffled Pillow

Finished Size: 24" x 12" (61 cm x 30 cm)

SHOPPING LIST

Yardage is based on 43"/44" (109 cm/112 cm) wide fabric with a usable width of 40" (102 cm).

- ☐ 7/8 yd (80 cm) of floral print fabric for pillow front and back
- ☐ 1/2 yd (46 cm) of chevron stripe fabric for ruffle
- ☐ 7/8 yd (80 cm) of muslin fabric **and** polyester fiberfill to make pillow form **OR** a purchased 24" x 12" (61 cm x 30 cm) knife-edge pillow form

- ☐ 2 1/4 yds (2.1 m) of Wright's® Maxi Piping
- ☐ sewing machine zipper foot
- ☐ General Supplies (see page 28)

Fig. 1

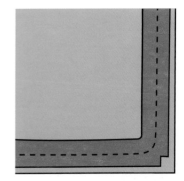

Fig. 2

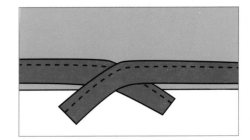

CUTTING THE PIECES

*Follow **Preparing Fabrics**, page 28, to prepare fabrics before cutting pieces. All measurements include 1/2" seam allowances.*

From floral print fabric:
- Cut **pillow front** and **pillow back** 25" x 13".

From chevron stripe fabric:
- Cut 4 **ruffle strips** 4" x 40".

From muslin fabric:
- Cut **pillow form front** and **pillow form back** 26" x 14".

MAKING THE PILLOW

Match right sides and use a 1/2" seam allowance unless otherwise indicated. Backstitch at beginning and ending of stitching line.

1. Attach zipper foot to sewing machine on right side of needle. Matching raw edges and beginning at center of one side of pillow front, sew piping to right side of **pillow front**, making a clip in the seam allowance to the basting at each corner of piping to allow it to lay flat (**Fig. 1**). Overlap ends as shown in **Fig. 2**; baste across overlap.

2. Matching short raw edges, join **ruffle strips**. Press seam allowances open. Press each short end to wrong side.

3. Matching **wrong** sides and raw edges, fold ruffle in half lengthwise; press.

4. Pleating as you go, fold and baste approximately 1/2" pleats along the raw edge of the ruffle (**Fig. 3**) until ruffle is approximately 76".

Fig. 3

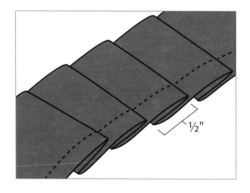

½"

5. Matching raw edges, pin ruffle to right side of pillow front over piping; overlap ruffle ends slightly.

6. Use a ³/₈" seam allowance to baste ruffle to pillow front.

7. Matching raw edges and leaving an opening for turning along 1 side, pin and stitch **pillow back** to pillow front, taking 2 stitches diagonally at each corner as shown in **Fig. 12**, page 31. Trim each corner as shown in **Fig. 13**, page 31. Turn pillow right side out; press.

8. If making a pillow form, refer to **Making A Pillow Form**, page 30.

9. Insert pillow form and close opening using the **Ladder Stitch**, page 31.

Box-Edge Pillow

Finished Size: 16" diameter (41 cm) with 3" (8 cm) deep sides

SHOPPING LIST

Yardage is based on 43"/44" (109 cm/112 cm) wide fabric with a usable width of 40" (102 cm). A fat quarter measures approximately 22" x 18" (56 cm x 46 cm).

- ☐ pink paisley print flannel fat quarter for wedges
- ☐ pink owl print flannel fat quarter for wedges
- ☐ blue dot print flannel fat quarter for wedges
- ☐ yellow floral print flannel fat quarter for side strips
- ☐ 2 green print flannel fat quarters for wedges and welting
- ☐ 4 assorted felt scraps
- ☐ $7/8$ yd (80 cm) of muslin fabric **and** polyester fiberfill to make pillow form
- ☐ 3 yds (2.7 m) of $4/32$" (3 mm) diameter cord
- ☐ two $1/2$" (13 mm) diameter neon pom-poms
- ☐ sewing machine zipper foot
- ☐ hot glue gun and glue sticks
- ☐ 6" (15 cm) upholstery needle
- ☐ extra strong upholstery thread
- ☐ cellophane tape
- ☐ tracing paper
- ☐ General Supplies (see page 28)

MAKING THE PILLOW

Match right sides and use $1/2$" seam allowances unless otherwise indicated. Backstitch at beginning and ending of stitching line.

1. Sew 4 **wedges** (1 of each fabric) together. Sew 4 more wedges (1 of each fabric) together in same color order. Sew two sections together to make pillow front; press seam allowances open. Repeat to make pillow back.

2. Use pillow front as pattern to cut pillow form front and pillow form back from muslin; set aside.

3. Fold pillow front in half from top to bottom, then fold in half from left to right. At raw edges, make a $1/4$" clip at each fold. Repeat for pillow back.

4. Sew **side strips** together end to end; press seam allowances open. Cut strip $51\frac{1}{2}$" long. Sew ends together to make a loop.

CUTTING THE PIECES

*Follow **Preparing Fabrics**, page 28, to prepare fabrics before cutting pieces. All measurements include seam allowances.*

From pink paisley print fat quarter:
- Trace pattern, page 27, onto tracing paper. Using pattern, cut 2 **wedges**.

From pink owl print fat quarter:
- Using pattern, cut 2 **wedges**.

From blue dot print fat quarter:
- Using pattern, cut 2 **wedges**.

From yellow floral print fat quarter:
- Cut 3 **side strips** 4" x 20".

From 1 green print fat quarter:
- Using pattern, cut 4 **wedges**.

From felt scraps:
- Trace patterns, page 27, onto tracing paper. Using patterns, cut 2 **flowers** of each size.

From muslin:
- Cut 2 pillow form **sides** 4" x 40".

5. Fold loop in half. At both raw edges, make a ¹/₄" clip at each fold (**Fig. 1**); set aside.

Fig. 1

6. Use remaining fat quarter and follow **Making and Attaching Welting**, page 29, to make 2 bias strips 1³/₄" x 54", to make welting, and to attach welting to pillow front and pillow back. Leave zipper foot on sewing machine.

7. Matching right sides, raw edges, and clips, sew one edge of sides to pillow front over welting.

8. Sew remaining edge to pillow back in the same manner, leaving an opening for turning. Clip seam allowances about every ¹/₂". Turn pillow right side out; press.

9. Refer to **Making A Pillow Form**, page 30, using muslin pillow form front, back, and sides.

10. Insert pillow form and close opening using the **Ladder Stitch**, page 31.

11. Thread needle with a length of upholstery thread; knot ends together. Stack 1 of each **flower** in center of pillow front and pillow back. Run needle through center of the flowers and pillow from front to back; run needle back through flowers and pillow. Pull thread tightly to bring pillow front and back together. Repeat several times. Secure and clip thread.

12. Glue 1 pom-pom to center of each flower.

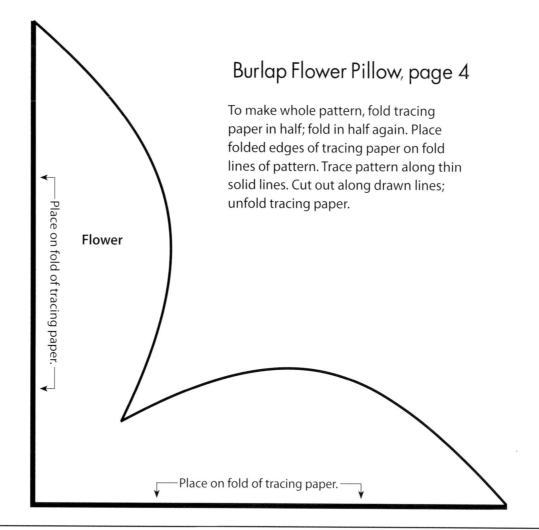

Burlap Flower Pillow, page 4

To make whole pattern, fold tracing paper in half; fold in half again. Place folded edges of tracing paper on fold lines of pattern. Trace pattern along thin solid lines. Cut out along drawn lines; unfold tracing paper.

Place on fold of tracing paper.

Flower

Place on fold of tracing paper.

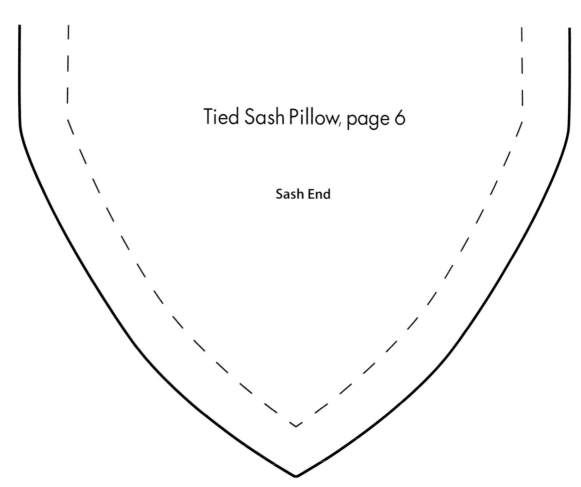

Tied Sash Pillow, page 6

Sash End

Patterns

Welted Bolster Pillow, page 8

To make whole pattern, fold tracing paper in half; fold in half again. Place folded edges of tracing paper on fold lines of pattern. Trace pattern along thin solid lines. Cut out along drawn lines; unfold tracing paper.

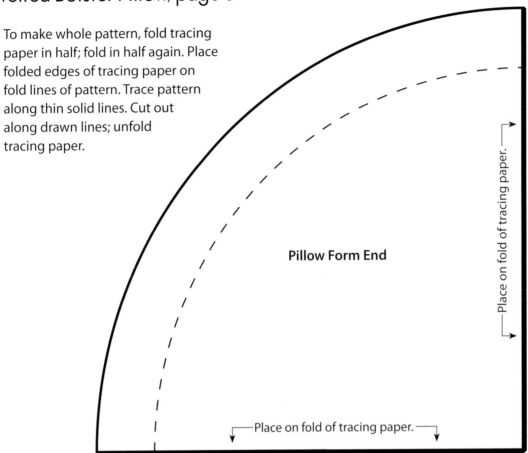

Pillow Form End

Place on fold of tracing paper.

Place on fold of tracing paper.

Tied Bolster Pillow, page 12

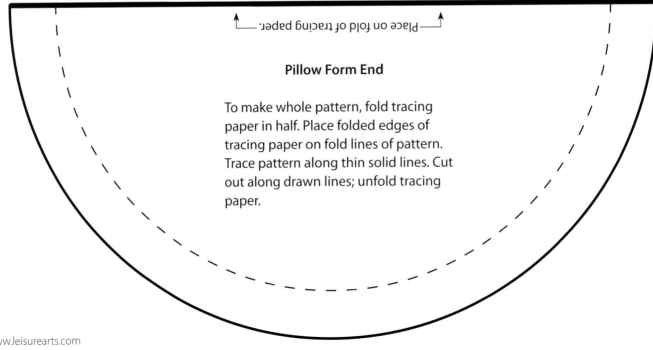

Place on fold of tracing paper.

Pillow Form End

To make whole pattern, fold tracing paper in half. Place folded edges of tracing paper on fold lines of pattern. Trace pattern along thin solid lines. Cut out along drawn lines; unfold tracing paper.

Round Welted Pillow, page 14

To make whole pattern, fold paper in half; fold in half again. Fold paper in half again. Place folded edges of paper on fold lines of pattern. Trace pattern along curved line. Cut out along drawn line; unfold paper.

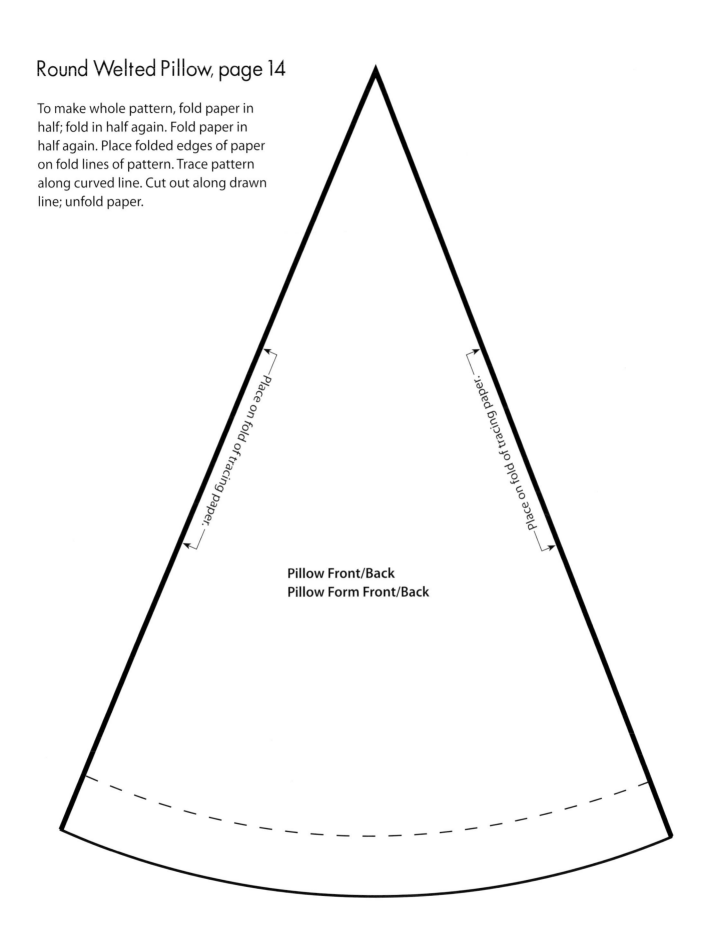

Place on fold of tracing paper.

Place on fold of tracing paper.

Pillow Front/Back
Pillow Form Front/Back

It is Well with my Soul

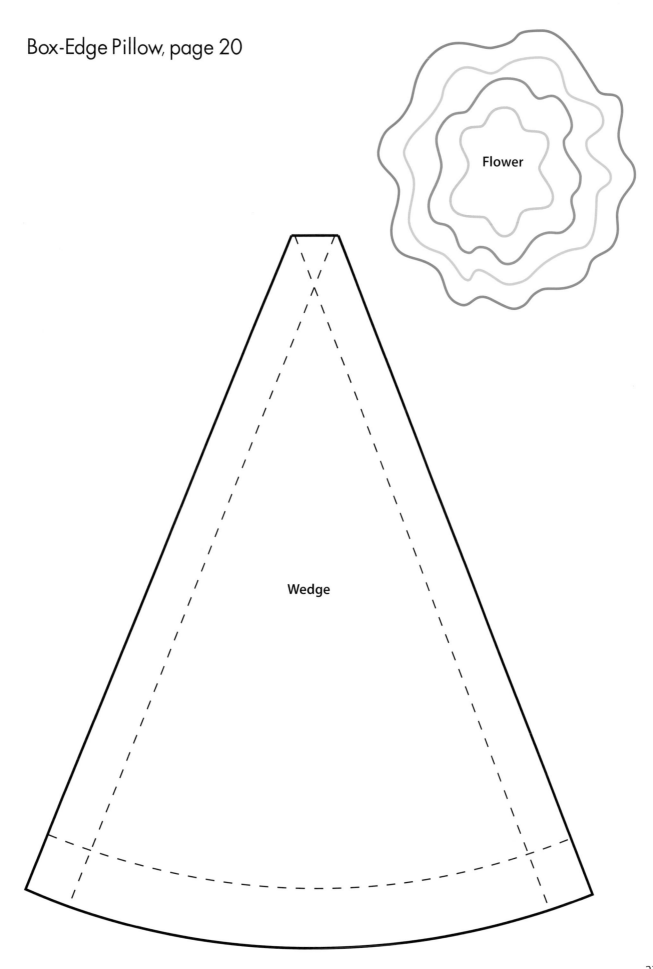

Flower

Wedge

GENERAL SUPPLIES

- ☐ fabrics - Refer to **Selecting Fabrics** and individual project shopping list.

- ☐ 15" or larger square clear plastic rotary cutting ruler with grid **or** carpenter's square

- ☐ yardstick

- ☐ marking tools - #2 pencil, fabric marking pen, or tailor's chalk

- ☐ pressing cloth - optional; suggested when ironing fabrics to protect the finish

- ☐ additional supplies are required; these are listed with individual projects

SELECTING FABRICS

The type of fabric you choose depends on how the pillow will be used and where it will be placed in your home. Photography models were made from lightweight cotton fabric, heavy cotton duck, burlap, flannel, home decorating fabric, and upholstery fabric. Check labels on fabric bolts for care instructions.

Consider buying quality fabrics, as they are easier to work with and the end results will be more pleasing. Ask your store sales clerk if you need assistance in locating fabrics that would be suitable for the projects in this book. Allow extra fabric for one-way designs or large patterns.

PREPARING FABRICS

If your pillow will require washing or dry cleaning, wash or dry clean your fabric before cutting out pieces. This will preshrink the fabric and remove any excess dye. But be aware that washing some fabrics may dull the shiny finish. We do not recommend prewashing burlap because of excess fraying.

Knowing the basics of fabric grain is essential to cutting fabric pieces correctly; cutting fabric pieces on grain eliminates stretching and puckering of the finished pillow. Grain refers to the direction of threads woven in the fabric. Selvage refers to the finished edge of woven fabric. Crosswise grain refers to the threads running the width of the fabric from selvage to selvage. Lengthwise grain refers to the threads running the length of the fabric, parallel to the selvages. Bias refers to the diagonal direction on a piece of fabric in relation to crosswise and lengthwise grain (**Fig. 1**).

Fig. 1

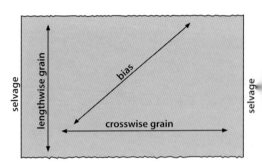

Before cutting out pieces for your pillow, it is important that the cut edges of your fabric are straight or "squared." Matching right sides and selvages, fold fabric in half; press. Refer to **Fig. 2** and place a square ruler or carpenter's square on fabric, with one edge aligned with selvages and an adjacent edge close to bottom of fabric. Mark a straight line along bottom edge of ruler; move ruler and continue line to fold. Cut fabric along drawn line.

Fig. 2

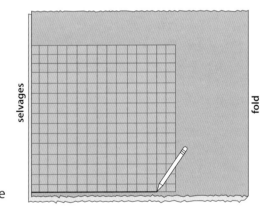

For pattern fabrics with designs that are printed slightly off-grain, the finished pillow will look better if you square the fabric along the pattern design instead of the crosswise grain. Lay fabric flat. Using one edge of a square ruler or carpenter's square, draw a line across bottom edge of fabric from selvage to selvage, following the pattern rather than the grain. Cut fabric along drawn line.

Individual project instructions indicate size to cut fabric pieces for pillow. Start from squared edge when measuring and cutting pieces.

MAKING AND ATTACHING WELTING

Welting is synthetic or cotton cord covered with a bias fabric strip and has an outside seam allowance for stitching into a seam.

When working with cord, it will be helpful to wrap each end with cellophane tape to prevent unraveling. When trimming cord, wrap tape around cord where it will be cut, then cut through tape.

Fabric strips cut on the bias stretch easily. Using bias strips to cover your cord will allow the welting to turn neat, smooth corners and curves around your pillow.

1. To find bias of fabric, refer to **Fig. 3** and lay fabric wrong side up; fold one corner of fabric diagonally so that lengthwise grain aligns with crosswise grain. Press fold, being careful not to stretch fabric. Cut fabric along fold.

Fig. 3

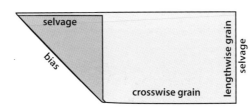

2. Individual project instructions indicate width and total length of bias strip needed for welting. Bias strips will need to be cut and pieced until required length is obtained. With lines spaced apart the specified width, mark lines on wrong side of fabric parallel to bias edge (**Fig. 4**).

Fig. 4

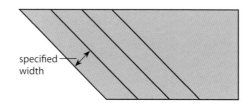

3. Cut strips apart. Matching right sides, pin two strips together; points should extend equal distances beyond overlap. Stitch strips together (**Fig. 5**). Press seam allowances open; trim points. Repeat to join additional strips until pieced strip is required length.

Fig. 5

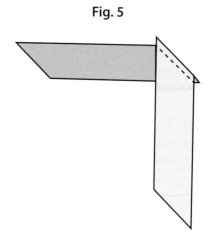

4. Attach zipper foot to sewing machine on right side of needle. Center cord on wrong side of bias strip. Matching long raw edges, fold bias strip over cord; pin. Referring to **Fig. 6** and gently stretching fabric as you stitch, baste next to cord. Leave zipper foot on sewing machine.

Fig. 6

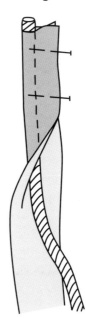

5. Matching raw edges and beginning at center of one side of pillow front, pin welting to right side of pillow front, making a clip in the seam allowance to the basting at each corner of welting to allow it to lay flat. Ends of welting should overlap 2"; pin overlapping end out of the way (**Fig. 7**).

Fig. 7

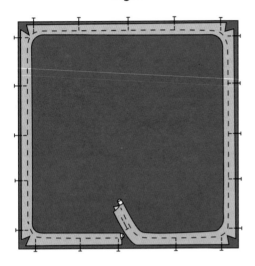

6. Beginning 2" from the beginning end of welting, baste welting to pillow front along basting line of welting, taking two stitches diagonally at each corner as shown in **Fig. 12**; stop 4" from overlapped end of welting (**Fig. 8**).

Fig. 8

7. Trim overlapping end of welting so that it overlaps beginning end by 1$^1/_4$". Use seam ripper to remove 2" of basting from overlapping end of welting; pull end of cord out and cut off 1$^1/_4$" (**Fig. 9**). This will make ends of cord meet. Tape ends of cord together.

Fig. 9

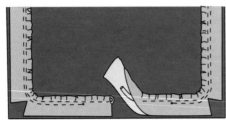

8. On overlapped end of fabric strip, fold end of fabric under $^1/_2$" (**Fig. 10**); wrap this end of fabric over other end of welting; pin in place. Finish basting welting to pillow front (**Fig. 11**).

Fig. 10

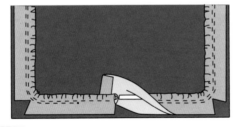

Fig. 11

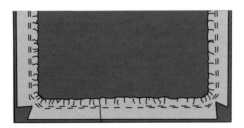

9. Follow individual project instructions to complete pillow.

MAKING A PILLOW FORM

(**Note:** Use a $^1/_2$" seam allowance. Backstitch at beginning and ending of stitching line.)

1. Individual project instructions indicate size to cut two pieces of muslin for pillow form. Matching right sides and raw edges, pin and stitch **pillow form front** to **pillow form back**, taking two stitches diagonally at each corner as shown in **Fig. 12** and leaving an 8" opening on one side for turning and stuffing. Trim each corner as shown in **Fig. 13**.

2. Turn form right side out. Press pillow form, folding seam allowances at opening to inside and pressing each fold to a sharp crease.

3. Stuff form firmly with polyester fiberfill, completely filling in corners before stuffing remainder of form. Close opening using the **Ladder Stitch** (**Fig. 14**).

TUFTING

1. Thread needle with a length of extra strong upholstery thread; knot ends together. Securely knot end of thread through 1 button or around the shank of 1 button.
2. Run needle through pillow, then through holes or shank of second button; run needle back through pillow and through first button. Pull thread tightly.
3. Repeat Step 2 several times. Secure and clip thread.

SEWING CORNERS

Taking two diagonal stitches across a corner as shown in **Fig. 12** creates a well-formed point when the pillow is turned right side out.

Fig. 12

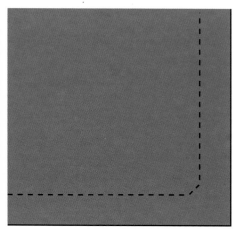

TRIMMING CORNERS

To reduce bulk at a corner, trim seam allowances diagonally approximately $1/8$" from stitching; then, taper seam allowances on each side **(Fig. 13)**.

Fig. 13

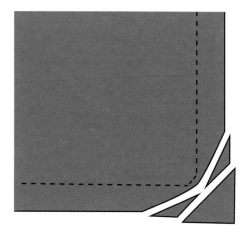

LADDER STITCH

This stitch is used for joining two folded edges of fabric without leaving visible stitches. Knot thread end; bring needle out through folded edge at 1. Insert needle in opposite folded edge at 2. Push needle through fold approximately $1/8$"; bring needle out at 3. Continue in this manner, alternating from one folded edge to the other **(Fig. 14)**.

Fig. 14

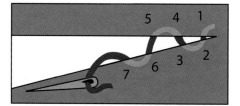

Meet Billie Steward

Billie Steward enjoys sewing "anything for the home" but says pillows and custom-fit slipcovers are her favorite projects.

"I love making pillows because you can get so creative," she says. "I love a lot of different styles, but French farmhouse has to be my favorite."

A former designer and technical writer for Leisure Arts, Billie says she received her love for design and her ability to create what she sees in her mind from her mother.

"About 17 years ago, I was asked by an interior designer friend if I would make a few pillows for a client of hers. Of course I said yes and that job led to another which then led to my custom slipcover business."

Her designs have appeared in several Arkansas home decorating and lifestyle magazines.

Billie now works full time at a gift shop, teaches dance cardio classes two nights a week, and spends her spare time doting on her four cats or relaxing at nearby Greer's Ferry Lake.

Metric Conversion Chart

Inches x 2.54 = centimeters (cm)
Inches x 25.4 = millimeters (mm)
Inches x .0254 = meters (m)

Yards x .9144 = meters (m)
Yards x 91.44 = centimeters (cm)
Centimeters x .3937 = inches (")
Meters x 1.0936 = yards (yd)

Standard Equivalents

1/8"	3.2 mm	0.32 cm	1/8 yard	11.43 cm	0.11 m
1/4"	6.35 mm	0.635 cm	1/4 yard	22.86 cm	0.23 m
3/8"	9.5 mm	0.95 cm	3/8 yard	34.29 cm	0.34 m
1/2"	12.7 mm	1.27 cm	1/2 yard	45.72 cm	0.46 m
5/8"	15.9 mm	1.59 cm	5/8 yard	57.15 cm	0.57 m
3/4"	19.1 mm	1.91 cm	3/4 yard	68.58 cm	0.69 m
7/8"	22.2 mm	2.22 cm	7/8 yard	80 cm	0.8 m
1"	25.4 mm	2.54 cm	1 yard	91.44 cm	0.91 m

Production Team: Technical Writer – Lisa Lancaster; Technical Associate – Mary Sullivan Hutcheson; Editorial Writer – Susan Frantz Wiles; Senior Graphic Artist – Lora Puls; Graphic Artist – Victoria Temple; Photostylist – Lori Wenger; Photographer – Jason Masters.